Sormany Silva Dantas

Use of VisuAlg by students in introductory programming courses

Sormany Silva Dantas

Use of VisuAlg by students in introductory programming courses

Evaluation of the technical and pedagogical criteria that accredit the tool as didactic educational software

ScienciaScripts

Imprint

Any brand names and product names mentioned in this book are subject to trademark, brand or patent protection and are trademarks or registered trademarks of their respective holders. The use of brand names, product names, common names, trade names, product descriptions etc. even without a particular marking in this work is in no way to be construed to mean that such names may be regarded as unrestricted in respect of trademark and brand protection legislation and could thus be used by anyone.

Cover image: www.ingimage.com

This book is a translation from the original published under ISBN 978-613-9-65328-7.

Publisher:
Sciencia Scripts
is a trademark of
Dodo Books Indian Ocean Ltd. and OmniScriptum S.R.L publishing group

120 High Road, East Finchley, London, N2 9ED, United Kingdom
Str. Armeneasca 28/1, office 1, Chisinau MD-2012, Republic of Moldova, Europe
Printed at: see last page
ISBN: 978-620-7-86675-5

To my wife Lana for her strength and encouragement in not letting me give up in difficult times. To my children Gabriel and Anna Lys for being the reason for my struggle. To my grandparents João and Ana for giving me the character and honour necessary to build a man. To my dear mother Da Guia for her marvellous upbringing, affection, care, dedication and sensitivity. To my sister Danielli for her companionship and affection.

I love you all!

Summary

DANTAS, Sormany Silva. **Evaluation of educational software to support learning programming: VisuAlg.** Monograph presented to the Computing Degree course at the State University of Paraíba (UEPB). 2012. 44 pages.

The aim of this work is to assess the quality of VisuAlg software using the Reeves model (1994), with subjective application of its criteria, and the ISO/IEC 9126 technical standard, applied empirically. Based on the criteria and measures belonging to these two models, the aim of this work is to assess whether VisuAlg can be indicated as educational software, rather than a pedagogical solution for the teaching-learning process, since external factors such as the changing educational context directly interfere with the result. As the software is designed to support the learning of programming for beginners in programming language subjects, we chose to select the criteria that most closely match the context of the software. Thus, this work is exploratory in nature, using a non-probabilistic, intentional sample, through which observation was directed towards a case study of software to support the teaching of algorithms. As a result, we identified that, in terms of technical criteria, although it had reservations in two of the five criteria analysed, the result of the technical evaluation of the software was satisfactory. As for the pedagogical criteria, the software meets the requirements proposed by the study model used in the research, since it tends to facilitate and motivate learning of programming subjects.

Keywords: support learning, teach algorithms, motivate learning

Contents

CHAPTER 1

Introduction

Although in practice the evaluation of *software* is eminently a subjective activity of total acceptance or rejection, knowledge of the characteristics that make it suitable or not for the teaching-learning process, the interaction modalities it establishes with the user and its interrelationship with educational objectives in specific teaching situations, form a set of fundamental importance for the success of the relationship between information technology and education (BRANDÃO, 1998, p. 2).

When people talk about education and IT, they always refer to educational *software* that has been developed using programming languages, artificial intelligence principles and virtual reality. With this ever-increasing demand, it is necessary to verify the impact of these technologies on the educational process and establish criteria for making these choices, in order to define the most coherent characteristics relating to the quality of the *software*. *In other* words, when trying to classify whether educational *software* is good or not, one must think about what role these technologies play in education and what importance their use has for society (BRANDÃO, 1998).

1.1 *Software* concepts and their importance in the information society

Computer *software* has been advancing for a long time in various fields of activity around the world. This technology has become indispensable in business management, scientific studies and engineering development,

thus enabling the creation of new technologies, the extension of existing ones and, consequently, the decline of old technologies. This makes it easy to understand the importance of *software* today, as it takes on both the role of product and the vehicle that delivers this product. In the role of product, *software* generates, modifies, displays and transmits information, regardless of current computing power, whether in large *hardware* or small mobile phone handsets. As a vehicle, *software* is present from the low level, controlling *hardware* with operating systems and managing communication through networks, to the high level, with the creation and control of tools, programmes and *software* environments (PRESSMAN, 2006, p. 2).

Also according to Pressman (2006, p. 2), *software* has acquired a significant importance due to the way in which information is transformed into useful data within a given context and the way in which it is organised, improving competitiveness between organisations and providing the means to obtain this information in all its forms.

Associating *software* with a computer programme is the most likely and also the most simplistic view of the subject, but it does not contemplate its formal definition, which is precisely described by Sommerville (2007) when he says that:

> *Software* is not just the programme, but also all the associated documentation and configuration data needed for the programme to operate correctly. A *software* system usually consists of a set of separate programmes; configuration files, which are used to configure these programmes; system documentation, which describes the structure of the system; user documentation, which explains how to use the system; and *websites* through which users obtain recent information about the product (2007, p. 4).

This is why *software* allows us to watch TV, talk on the phone, surf the Internet, exchange messages with people on the other side of the world and, fundamentally, with the acquisition of information, we can carry out research and studies on any topic we want (TAKAHASHI, 2000, p. 3).

Takahashi (2000, p. 45) also emphasises that, with the advance of Information and

Communication Technologies (ICT), "*software has* found a way into environments where competence is needed to transform information into knowledge. Education is the key element in building a society based on information, knowledge and learning". In other words, technologies must integrate the community and the school so that education mobilises society and becomes the main objective to be achieved.

1.2   Software at school for pedagogical purposes

According to Valente (1999, p. 104), "the qualitative evaluation of educational *software* requires a thorough analysis, as it demands special attention with regard to the *software*'s theoretical-pedagogical foundation". Thus, working with *software* in schools allows students to experience things with fewer abstractions, to interfere in the results of these experiences, thus allowing them to build and promote their own knowledge by participating dynamically in educational action, interacting with the methods and means of organising their knowledge (AGUIAR, 2008, p. 1).

Therefore, finding *software to* help or complement teachers' teaching in classrooms or computer labs has become a more frequent practice in recent years, but it is far from a fact. However, this *software has* emerged with a pedagogical proposal to improve the quality of teaching within educational institutions (AGUIAR, 2008, p. 2). However, it is necessary to realise that the singular application of *software* is no guarantee of improved teaching quality. Choosing the right *software* depends on variables that must be analysed and studied before final submission (FERREIRA, MOREIRA, & MOZZAQUATRO, 2011, p. 1).

1.3   You need to check the quality of the *software*

Before including software to support educational processes, it is necessary to analyse the most appropriate way to insert these resources into the school environment, in an attempt to reduce possible resistance or deviations from the objective of using them. The process of qualitatively evaluating a piece of *software* suggests choosing prerequisites that underpin a quality standard with the aim of analysing whether "the reality that the *software* suggests is consistent with a model that aims to be ideal based on the educational paradigm for the target audience for which the *software is* intended". Even so, before judging whether or not the software is appropriate to fulfil its role, caution is needed, as it is necessary to foresee what the real role of these technologies is in the students' educational process (RAMOS, 2003, p. 1).

However, the qualitative analysis of the *software* and its subsequent classification as educational implies a meticulous approach, given the variety of existing *software* and the specificity that each one has in terms of its theoretical-pedagogical foundation. According to Valente (1999):

> It is necessary to look at the *software*'s specifications in terms of the target audience, how it is used, the support materials needed to use the *software,* how the content is presented (consistency and structure) and how it stimulates creativity, imagination, reasoning, group work and the user's level of involvement (1999, p. 111).

However, it is not easy to choose a methodology and apply it to analysing software with the sole purpose of classifying it. The complexity intrinsic to the evaluation process is real, and the determining variable for its success depends on the context to which the *software* will be submitted. Silva and Vargas (1999) are spot on in this respect when they state that "knowing or determining the quality and effectiveness of educational *software* is a complex task due to the various domains of human behaviour involved in the interaction".

The complexity required by the assessment process, combined with other factors, can be a determining factor in the reluctance of educators and school managers to adapt to the new educational paradigm. This new model points to the need for educators to adapt not only to the inclusion of these technologies in their daily lives, but, above all, to be part of the choice of *software* that can streamline the evolutionary teaching-learning process. Since there is no one better qualified to observe the context of the school institution, which conditions learning theories by making them distinct educational environments. (SILVA & VARGAS, 1999, p. 3)

From this moment on, educational *software is* treated as a tool, an instrument that helps and motivates the practical pedagogical process, providing the means to plan "simple and creative situations and activities, thus providing positive results in the assessment of their students and their work, [...] only in this way will the process of computerisation of society become effectively irreversible" (LUCENA, 1998).

In this sense, the basis for this work came from a literature search on the topic of Information Technology in Education, which found works that only mention Reeves' methods and the ISO/IEC 9126 standard in little detail. In these works, the focus is on technical and development criteria. Therefore, the lack of an evaluation, mainly of a pedagogical nature concomitant with technical criteria, motivated us to carry out this study.

1.4 General objective

To evaluate the VisuAlg *software based* on Thomas Reeves' pedagogical model (1994) and the ISO/IEC 9126 standard, providing a list of aspects that can be observed in educational *software.* Complementary phases were developed to fulfil the general objective through the following specific objectives:

1.5 Specific objectives

The specific objectives related to the general objective are as follows:

- Demonstrate the *software* evaluation methodologies used in the study;

- Introducing the VisuAlg *software* and other similar systems;

- Identify the points assessed by Reeves' pedagogical methodology;

- Define the evaluation criteria for the ISO/IEC 9126 standard.

1.6 Methodology

This is a descriptive exploratory study. According to Gil (2006), descriptive research has the primary objective of describing the characteristics of a given population or phenomenon, or establishing relationships between variables. According to Marconi and Lakatos (2007), exploratory studies are those that aim to fully describe a particular phenomenon. The sample chosen was non-probabilistic and intentional, i.e. the research was aimed at a case study of *software to* support the teaching of algorithms.

Firstly, a bibliographical survey was carried out in order to obtain the necessary knowledge to develop a contextualisation, arguments and observations, ensuring the quality of the information. Then, after analysing the studies, Reeves' pedagogical model was chosen because it presents two relevant characteristics to be observed in educational *software:*

- Comprehensive: composed of 14 criteria that assess the pedagogical conceptions of learning objects; and

- Flexible: which allows the model to be used partially, choosing only the criteria that most identify with the objects to be evaluated.

The pedagogical evaluation will be carried out by checking the tendency that the *software* will show in relation to the pedagogical conception analysed, and it is up to the evaluator to subjectively classify each criterion, checking compliance with the use of the *software*. The conceptions are analysed using a graphic procedure, on a non-dimensional scale represented by a double arrow. At the ends of the arrows are the opposing concepts, with the most negative on the left and the most positive on the right. The assessment is concluded by analysing the arrangement of the points marked on the arrows, which must be connected by placing the arrows on top of each other, as shown in Figure 1.1, followed by the details of the assessment.

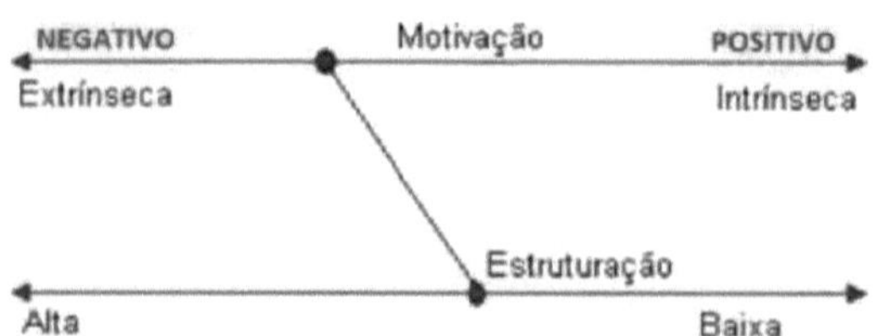

Figure 1.1: Graphical procedure in Reeves Bertoldi's methodology (1999).

As for the technical standard, the choice was justified by the set of characteristics and sub-characteristics that define product quality and can be applied to any *software*. The quality assessment will be verified by subjecting each set to specific, targeted tests on the *software* and observing the conformity between the sub-characteristics. At the end of the analysis, these classifications will determine the product's quality level. Then, based on the results obtained and the observation of the educational aspects provided by the application of the study, the pedagogical definition of the *software* will be presented.

CHAPTER 2

Theoretical Framework

This section will discuss some theoretical assumptions that are relevant to understanding the proposed objective, highlighting evaluation models and methods, along with the technical standards that help produce *software,* other similar systems that support the learning of programming languages, emphasising the VisuAlg study object, the pedagogical evaluation model proposed by Reeves and the ISO/IEC 9126 technical standard for evaluating *software* quality.

2.1   Evaluation of educational *software*

When developing and evaluating the quality of a learning object[1] two important aspects need to be investigated: learning and usability. The evaluation of learning deals with pedagogical problems, logic, the interest of the objectives, perceptibility and, above all, proof of student learning and the need to improve the teaching-learning process. The usability assessment addresses ergonomic problems related to the student's adaptation to the *software. In* this way, students will reach their goals more quickly, with less effort and more satisfaction. In other words, *software* with good usability will lead to learning that is efficient, productive and effective (GAMA, 2007, p. 20).

Within the pedagogical assessment process, Gama (2007) highlights two perspectives: the

---

[1] Learning Objects can be defined as any entity, digital or non-digital, that can be used, reused or referenced during technology-supported learning.

formative, which acts continuously and progressively throughout the teaching-learning process in order to improve it, investigating practical learning and analysing the student's behaviour, interest and participation, all of which favours the development of didactics adapted to the student; while summative evaluates the final process and is designed to offer conclusions about the instructional *design* as a whole. The student is graded by assigning a mark, where theoretical learning is ascertained.

In general terms, we can describe some models and methods that have been developed by Brazilians who are looking for mechanisms to evaluate educational *software,* and international scholars who carry out research aimed at analysing learning objects, as cited by Gama (2007, p. 35):

- **The LORI** *(Learning Object Review Instruments)* **evaluation tool** developed by *e-Leaming Research and Assessment,* LORI is a facilitating guide for analysing the quality of a learning object made available on the Internet. It has nine evaluation criteria: content quality, learning object alignment, *feedback* and adaptation, motivation, presentation design, usability, accessibility, reusability and adherence to standards. It uses a scoring scale that ranges from one (lowest) to five (highest). It is widely used in work carried out in Canada and the United States (GAMA, 2007, pp. 44-45);

- **Thomas Reeves Methodology:** based on pedagogical criteria (epistemology, pedagogical philosophy, underlying psychology, objectivity, instructional sequencing, experimental validity, the role of the instructor, valuing error, motivation, structure, accommodation of individual differences, student control, user activity and co-operative learning) and user interface criteria (ease of use, navigation, cognitive load, mapping, screen *design,* spatial compatibility of knowledge, presentation of information, integration of media, aesthetics and general functionality). It has no evaluation scale. This procedure is entirely subjective (GAMA, 2007, pp. 38-41);

- **Martins' methodology:** aims to analyse the interactions between the student, the *web* interface and the teaching material in order to see to what extent this interaction favours learning. It also assesses whether the students are able to achieve their objectives in terms of enjoyable learning. The ergonomic properties are analysed in detail and its usability addressed from two aspects: *design* and pedagogy. It uses a specific form based on Jakob Nielsen's (2004) ten heuristics: *feedback,* speaking the user's language, clearly demarcated outputs, consistency, preventing errors, minimising the user's memory overload, shortcuts, simple and natural dialogues, good error messages and help and documentation (GAMA, 2007, pp. 41-42);

- **Ally & Krauss Methodology:** defends the constructivist learning theory. It uses three assessment strategies: recognising the environment, assessing the quality of learning objects using the LORI assessment tool and distributing a questionnaire to check the impact of learning using learning objects (GAMA, 2007, pp. 46-47);

- **Field Evaluation Model:** follows the form of a manual for the evaluation of educational *software in* which the objectives determine the general properties that the product to be evaluated must possess. The factors are responsible for the quality of the product and the criteria used to verify the quality of the *software.* There is a need for a multidisciplinary team to analyse the quality of the *software,* including IT professionals, educational professionals and the students themselves. According to the model, *software* quality is determined by the objectives: reliability of representation, usability and conceptual reliability; by the factors: legibility, manipulability, maintainability, operability, portability, reusability, efficiency, profitability, evaluability, reliability, integrity; and sub-factors: clarity, conciseness, style, modularity, availability, structure, traceability, timeliness, user-friendliness, accuracy, completeness, necessity, robustness and security (GAMA, 2007, pp. 42-44). 42-43);

- **Nesbit's Convergent Participation Model: a** model that develops in two compulsory cycles: in the first, the process is asynchronous and can last several days. The participants examine the object and submit it for individual evaluation using the LORI evaluation instrument; in the second, only one person takes part, who, using impartiality, manages the stage by initiating a discussion on the divergent results of the first cycle, reviewing them and ensuring that everyone reaches the same consensus. At the end of the second cycle, the moderator publishes the results revised by the participants (GAMA, 2007, p. 46);

- **The MERLOT Evaluation Model** *(Multimedia Educational Resource for Learning and Online Teaching) is* based on three dimensions: content quality, usability and potential as a teaching tool. It includes the pedagogical part of the process and its evaluation scale, which runs from 1 to 5, has the following values: 1) of no value for use; 2) does not meet the standards, but is of some use; 3) meets the standards, but presents risks; 4) very good, but with small risks; and 5) excellent in all aspects (GAMA, 2007, pp. 45-46);

- **TICESE Technique:** focuses on the development of the "Technique for Inspecting the Ergonomic Conformity of Educational *Software*" with the aim of developing the scientific bases that adapt working conditions to the capabilities and realities of those involved, guiding and providing theoretical and methodological parameters to aid the process of assessing the quality of educational *software* based on ergonomic and pedagogical issues from the

Ergolist tool[2] (GAMA, 2007, pp. 35-37);

- **Bloom's Taxonomy:** with a proposal for systematised assessment interpreted as an instrument, it has the task of classifying educational goals and objectives. The theory divides learning into domains and factors. The pedagogical domains are divided into mutually exclusive areas: the cognitive, which refers to understanding knowledge, application, synthesis and evaluation; the effective, which is directly linked to feelings and attitudes such as attitudes, responsibilities, respect, emotion and values; and the psychomotor, linked to physical actions. As for the factors, knowledge refers to the more specific part with an emphasis on memory processes; and comprehension refers to a type of understanding that is independent of the complexity of the material. Theory that leads to what educators want students to learn. It is useful in the application of assessment tests with a view to teaching content (GAMA, 2007, pp. 37-38).

If we add up the data described above, we can see that evaluating educational products creates major challenges for researchers and educators. The biggest is knowing whether a learning object or piece of software used for educational purposes is effective and whether it fulfils the basic requirements for quality teaching and learning. Many studies aimed at analysing these products confirm that there is insufficient knowledge about the models and methods that would make the process more interesting, given the complexity and variety of existing *software*. Based on the above, Gama (2007) indicates criteria that can be considered indispensable when seeking to effectively analyse educational *software*, which are classified into: pedagogical characteristics, ease of use, interface characteristics and adaptability.

Given this panorama, Thomaz (2005) presents a simple guideline on how to carry

---

[2] Available at http://www.labiutil.inf.ufsc.br/ergolist/

out an effective evaluation of educational *software.* Firstly, the objective and target audience (applicability) must be defined. Then you have to define the *software's* characteristics', select the criteria that apply to a particular piece of *software',* group these criteria according to their themes and objectives; particularise the criteria for each piece of *software according* to the organisation's educational philosophical principles; and carry out the weighted average after defining weights for each of the aforementioned criteria. Finally, the evaluation must be finalised and a conclusive analysis made.

As for the technical standards that help in the development and production of *software,* Sodré (2006) and Gama (3007) cite the main ones:

- **ISO/IEC 14598:** which deals with the *software* product evaluation process by presenting an overview and providing supporting information. It is made up of a set of six criteria: **overview** - clarifies general concepts of *software* quality and assessment', **planning and management** - guidance for assessment support functions, acquisition, control, development, being used to develop assessment plans; **process for developers** - organisation to develop a new product, internal quality; **process for acquirers** - used to acquire or reuse other *software* products, ascertain acceptance of a product; **process for assessors** - independent assessment; and **documentation of assessment modules** - guidance for documentation of assessment modules, quality model (SODRÉ, 2006, pp. 23-24);

- **ISO/IEC 9241: an** international standard that checks the ergonomics of computerised office work, with the aim of promoting safety and health for computer users, guaranteeing comfort and efficiency in computer operation. It consists of seventeen rules, eight of which are aimed at evaluating *software:* **dialogue principle -** adaptability, *feedback,* control, error tolerance, suitability for learning; **system**

usability - context of use, *hardware,* environmental aspects, usability measures; **visual presentation of information** - information on screens, windows, input and output areas; **user guidance** - supplementary information, online help, error management, *feedback* message', **menu dialogue style - menu** structure, navigation, menu selection and exercises; **command language dialogue - command** syntax structure, input and output representation; **direct manipulation dialogue** - appearance, manipulation of graphic objects; and **form-filling dialogue** - *feedback* input form structure, field navigation (GAMA, 2007, pp. 30-32);

- **ISO/IEC 9126:** international standard that refers to *software* product quality models, forming a set of criteria defined by characteristics and sub- characteristics that measure and evaluate *software* products. These are: **functionality** - suitability, accuracy, interoperability, conformity and security of access; **reliability** - maturity, fault tolerance, recoverability; **usability** - intelligibility, apprehensibility, operability; **efficiency** - behaviour in relation to time, behaviour in relation to resources; **portability** - adaptability, ability to be installed, conformity, ability to replace; and **maintainability** - analysability, modifiability, stability, testability (SODRÉ, 2006, p. 28).

In view of the situation presented, this process can be defined as "an organisation of procedures necessary to confirm that it complies with the goals established in its development phase". It is an artifice for classifying specific situations according to the pre-established parameters characteristic of all educational *software.* This makes it a complex task for educators. Identifying which theoretical conception guides the student's learning and how they construct their own knowledge are premises that the educator must have when undertaking this task. In this way, based on an educational theory, the assessment process allows educators to discover the educational vision of how they see student learning. To do this, the chosen criteria must be followed, which are the primitive attributes that can be verified and the measures that indicate the degree to which a given criterion is present within the *software* (Rocha and Campos 1993).

To evaluate the programme's pedagogical proposal, we adopted the methodology suggested by Reeves (1994), according to which the measures were applied in the form of a graph with a subjective analysis of each criterion in the following context: the closer the points are to the measure on the right, the more positive the evaluation, and the closer the points are to the measure on the left, the more negative.

For a technical evaluation, we followed the guidelines of the ISO/IEC 9126 standard, which provides criteria for investigating certain characteristics alongside the pedagogical analysis. The measures applied relate to the degree of satisfaction of each criterion assessed, labelled as low, medium and high.

The following is a brief list of systems that support the learning of programming languages similar to the VisuAlg object of study, which was chosen to be evaluated using the criteria for observation and discussion proposed in this work.

2.2   VisuAlg and other similar systems

At university level, the logical reasoning involved in programming subjects is quite complex, which ends up causing a high drop-out rate, as well as a high failure rate compared to other subjects at universities (Píccolo et. al 2010). In addition, the teacher also encounters numerous problems in the process of learning programming, including the difficulty of recognising the co-natural abilities of their students, presenting new techniques for solving problems, instigating the students' capacity for abstraction, among others (Nobre and Menezes 2002).

Among the existing tools that help with this and other programming learning processes, we can highlight some that work directly in teaching programming (Nobre and Menezes 2002). These include

- **RoboProf:** is an online teaching system that provides information through a set of closed topics and exercises, supporting an introductory programming course. It can be used to teach the syntax and semantics of a language, as well as programme design;

- **AIDE** *(Automated Interactive Design Editor): is* a menu-based system that allows students to understand a new project, modify an existing one, or automatically generate the basic structure of a system. It provides a problem description, structure specification, module description and programme skeleton. It aims to guide the stages of *software* development by specifying the structure and describing each of the system's modules;

- **PORTUGOL/PLUS:** is a support tool for teaching programming logic that uses pseudo-algorithmic language to describe the tasks to be carried out in order to solve problems. It has an algorithm editor where files are typed in and manipulated using a menu-driven interface, and a compiler for the environment, capable of checking the algorithm instructions and, if there are no errors, generating a programme in the Pascal language;

- **AMBAP:** is a system that promotes *software* environments using a simple language and a processor that allows the student to: build a programme using algorithmic language, execute and debug the code and have the opportunity to understand the concepts of variables, commands and recursion. By using a simulator, there are no initial concerns for the student in terms of implementation details linked to specific machine characteristics;

- **VisuAlg: a** tool that uses resources close to the reality of a programming language. It teaches the basic principles of structured programming, as well as reading variable values, *debugging* and monitoring programme execution step by step, allowing students to easily understand the components that make up programmes. Figure 2.1 shows the initial screen of the programme.

In this sense, it is advisable to design and use *software* that supports the learning of programming, as is the case with VisuAlg, *software* that was designed with the aim of

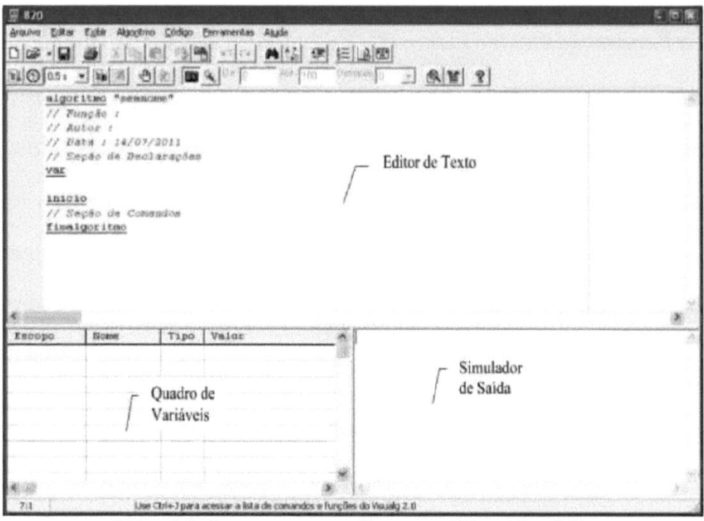

Figura 2.1:   VisuAlg home screen. Source: VisuAlg 2.0.

It also provides teaching resources that allow the teacher to better explain how the *software* works, such as: step-by-step execution, visualisation of the content of variables, examination of the activation stack in the case of subprograms, execution counter for each line of the programme. (Souza 2009). Figure 2.2 shows an example of pseudocode illustrating various features of the VisuAlg programming language.

The language used by the interpreter is one of the many variations of Portugol, widely used in computer science courses in Brazil. The syntax is similar to Pascal, but without the semicolon to separate commands. It uses a similar approach to BASIC, with one command per Node required, to make it easier to type and understand the pseudocode (Souza 2009).

According to Souza (2009, p. 8) the *software-*.facilitates understanding of how the computer programme works, provides immediate *feedback* on the correctness and accuracy of the pseudocode entered, and what is considered most important, encourages the student to experiment and see the result of their changes immediately.

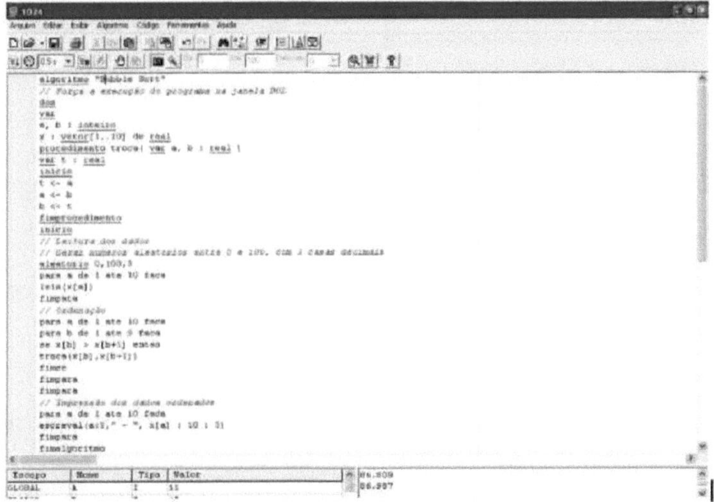

Figura 2.2:   Example of pseudocode in VisuAlg. Source: VisuAlg 2.0.

The programme can be executed in three ways: the standard mode, in which the pseudocode instructions are interpreted and executed immediately; the step-by-step mode, common to many development environments, in which the user commands the execution of the programme line by line, for debugging purposes or, in the case of VisuAlg, so that the student can examine the variables as their values change, perceive the processing flow in decision and repetition structures; and the animation mode, similar to the standard mode, with the difference that before the execution of a line of code there is a pause that can vary from 0.2 seconds to 5 seconds, which allows the student to follow the processing flow. Switching between these execution modes can be done via the main menu or toolbar, and also with commands included in the code, for example, the *timer on command switches* the animation *on,* and *timer off switches* it off. During the animation, any assignment of a value to a variable makes it visible and highlighted in the programme's "memory", helping to explain how loops, counters and accumulators work (Souza 2009).In the bottom left frame is the programme's memory, which stores the variables used in list form, with four columns that reference the variables: scope, name, type and value, as shown in Figure 2.3 below.

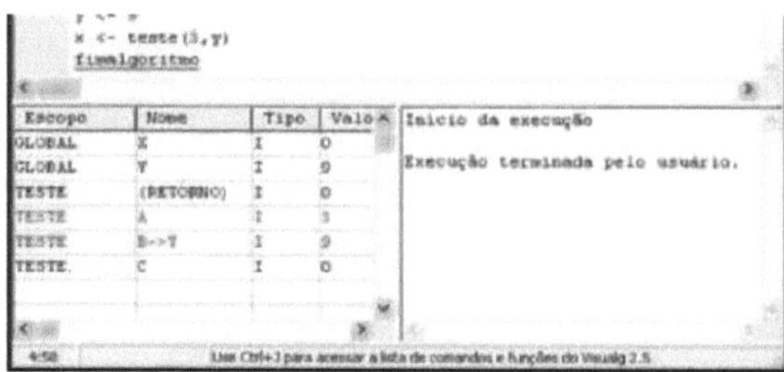

Figura 2.3:   Simulation of the memory of a running programme, below left. Source: VisuAlg 2.0.

Memory is a list containing the variables used in the programme and has four columns:

- Variable scope: can be global or local, in which case the name of the subroutine where it was declared is displayed;

- Variable name: in the case of elements in a vector, the name appears followed by the index or indices of the element, because in this list each one is considered a separate variable;

- Type of variable: character, integer, real or logical;

- Variable value.

The list of variables also uses different colouring depending on its use within the pseudocode:

- Variables declared in the VAR section are shown in black;

- Variables that represent parameters passed by value shown in green;

- Variables that represent parameters passed by reference are shown in red and the second column contains the name of the external variable to which it refers, i.e. the argument passed to the subprogramme;

- Variables that represent the return of a function are shown in blue and in place of the name is the expression (RETURN).

VisuAlg supports subroutines (procedures and functions) and allows the activation stack of these subroutines to be examined when execution is in step-by-step mode. This tool allows the teacher to illustrate the mechanism of subroutine calls and recursion, for example, as shown in Figure 5 (Souza 2009).

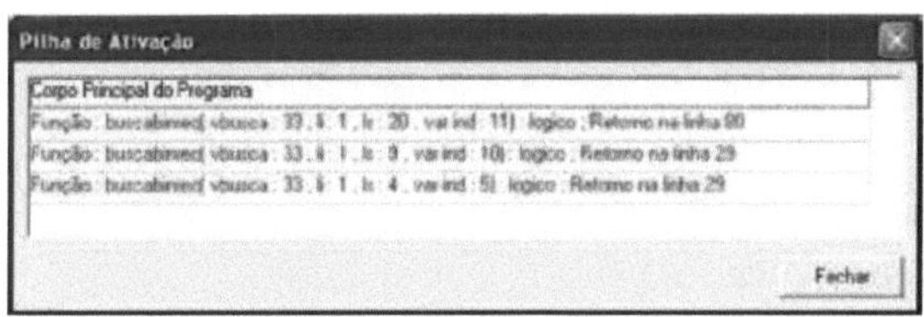

Figura 2.4:   Subroutine activation stack. Source: VisuAlg 2.0.

Often, in order to examine the efficiency of a solution to a problem, such as in sorting algorithms, it is necessary to know how many times a particular line of code has been executed. VisuAlg has a tool called Execution Profile, which allows you to check the statistics during the execution of a programme in step-by-step mode, or just after execution has finished. In it, the programme lines are displayed with their number, content and the number of times they have been executed, as shown in Figure 2.5.

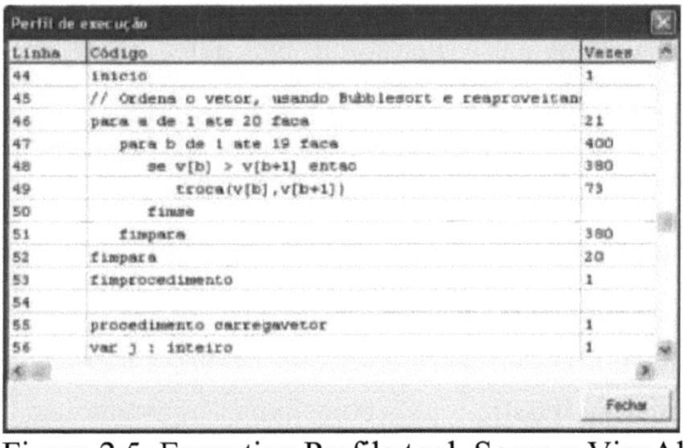

Figure 2.5: Execution Profile tool. Source: VisuAlg 2.0.

The author also emphasises the *software*'s effectiveness by stating that: "because it is written entirely in Portuguese and uses a model that is intuitive and familiar to students, it can be used in the very first programming lesson, without causing much impact". By making use of these benefits, students can focus on solving problems without having to master a programming language, while at the same time being introduced to concepts such as variable declarations and keywords. Other features such as: syntax similar to Pascal, but without the semicolon; an approach similar to BASIC, with one command per line to make typing easier; and an understanding of pseudocode, are additional benefits that make it easier for the student to understand.In view of this, two models will be used for the proposed assessment, which refer to technical and pedagogical criteria that will be explained later.

2.3   Reeves evaluation model

Reeves (1994) considers interactive multimedia to be a set of characteristics that can be described in different types of dimensions or criteria that evaluate pedagogical and interface conceptions. The interface criteria judge factors such as colour, text layout, animations and interactions and are concerned with ensuring that the student can really get involved in a significantly interactive process with the *software,* but the author himself considers that these interface criteria "are not sufficient to satisfy a complete analysis of educational *software*". Pedagogical criteria, on the other hand, are concerned with evaluating aspects of the *software's* design and implementation, which directly affect student learning and will serve as the basis for this study.

Frescki (2008) further defines the pedagogical criteria from Reeves (1994) that can be used as a basis for evaluating educational *software:*

- **Epistemology   [objectivist/constructivist]:**   in   objectivist   epistemology, knowledge is acquired objectively through the senses, with learning consisting of acquiring truths, while in constructivist epistemology, knowledge of reality is constructed individually, subjectively, based on reflections and previous experiences;

- **Pedagogical philosophy [instructivist/constructivist]:** instructivist is that which emphasises the importance of the student's independent goals, based on behaviourist theory, where the student is seen as a passive subject. Constructivist philosophy, on the other hand, emphasises interaction, strategy and the student's experience, where the student is seen as a passive subject.

an individual with knowledge and motivation;

- **Underlying psychology [behavioural/cognitive]:** behavioural means that the factors of learning are not behaviours that can be directly observed; instruction consists of modelling desirable behaviour obtained through stimulus-response. Cognitive is psychology that emphasises mental states rather than psychological behaviour. It recognises that a wide variety of learning strategies should be employed, taking into account the type of knowledge to be constructed;

- **Objectivity [precisely focussed/not focussed]:** precisely focussed is the form used in tutorials and training. Non-focussed is the form used in microworlds, virtual simulations and learning environments;

- **Instructional sequencing [reductionist/constructivist]:** it is reductionist when learning about a certain content requires all its components to be understood beforehand. It is constructivist when the student is placed in a realistic context, which will require problem-solving and support will be offered according to each user's individual needs;

- **Experimental Validity [abstract/concrete]:** it is abstract when situations are used that are not part of the student's reality. When it contextualises the content presented in real situations, it is concrete;

- **Role of the Instructor [material provider/facilitating agentj:** in the former, the instructor is considered the holder of knowledge, while in the latter he is seen as a source of guidance and consultation;

- **Valuing Error [learning without error/learning with experience]:** it is without error when the student is induced to answer the questions correctly. And with experience when it predicts that students will learn from their mistakes;

- **Motivation [extrinsic/intrinsic]:** it is extrinsic when it comes from outside the learning environment. It is intrinsic when the motivation comes from within;

- **Structuring [high/low]:** the *software is* highly structured when its sequence and paths have already been determined in advance. It has low structuring when the student can choose the order they want to follow in the *software',*

- **Accommodation of Individual Differences [does not exist/multifaceted]:** the former considers that all individuals are equal, the multifaceted considers the differences between subjects;

- **Student control [does not exist/unrestricted]:** does not exist when all control belongs to the *software,* and is unrestricted when the student decides which sessions to study, which paths to follow and which material to use. This criterion assesses the possibilities for the user to control the sequence and realisation of actions. This criterion refers to the fact that students should always be in control of system processing, such as interrupting, cancelling, suspending and continuing. Every possible user action should be anticipated and appropriate options offered;

- **User Activity [mathematical/generative]:** mathematical refers to learning environments where you want to enable the student to access the various representations of the content. Generative means that students are involved in a process of constructing or representing the content;

- **Cooperative Learning [unsupported/integral]:** unsupported when it does not allow work in pairs or groups, integral when it allows cooperative work, so that objectives are shared.

Therefore, the motivation for choosing this methodology is due to the fact that it comprises various criteria that can be fully involved in analysing the *software* or filtered down to the conceptions that need to be studied. With this flexibility, the methodology stands out compared to other models that are sometimes made up of complements to other assessment instruments, sometimes require more complex processes with more steps to achieve a result or are a mixture of observations, diverting the focus from pedagogical analysis. These characteristics were decisive in choosing the methodology that will guide the pedagogical evaluation of the educational **software.**

2.4 ISO/IEC 9126 standard

The concept of quality is defined by Sodré (2006) as being "a set of characteristics of every product and service or relationship that is planned, practised and verified, with the aim of exceeding the satisfaction expectations of the people involved". Quality is associated with the definition of conformity to specifications and the user's views of satisfaction; however, the following are also relevant factors for evaluation: deadlines, punctuality of delivery and flexibility (PMBOK, 2008).

Sodré (2006) states that this concept arose from the need to organise and standardise *software* development without planning or established quality standards. Before that, the only way to obtain an efficient system was through planning by the programmer himself. This quality can be divided into *software* process quality improvement and *software* product quality improvement. According to Sodré (2006), the ISO/IEC 9126-1 standard consists of a set of characteristics and sub-characteristics that define a quality product and can be applied to any *software product*. In Brazil it was launched in 1996 under a translated version called NBR 13596 and after several revisions and improvements, the standard was divided as follows:

- ISO/IEC 9126-1: Quality Model;

- ISO/IEC 9126-2: External Metrics;

- ISO/IEC 9126-3: Internal Metrics;

- ISO/IEC 9126-4: Quality Metrics in Use.

This model is made up of two parts: the Internal and External Quality Model and the Quality of Use Model, as shown in Figure 2.6.

Internal Quality is developed within a set of characteristics that involve the *software* product in an internal view, and is used to specify the properties of the intermediate *software* product. For its part, External Quality is also

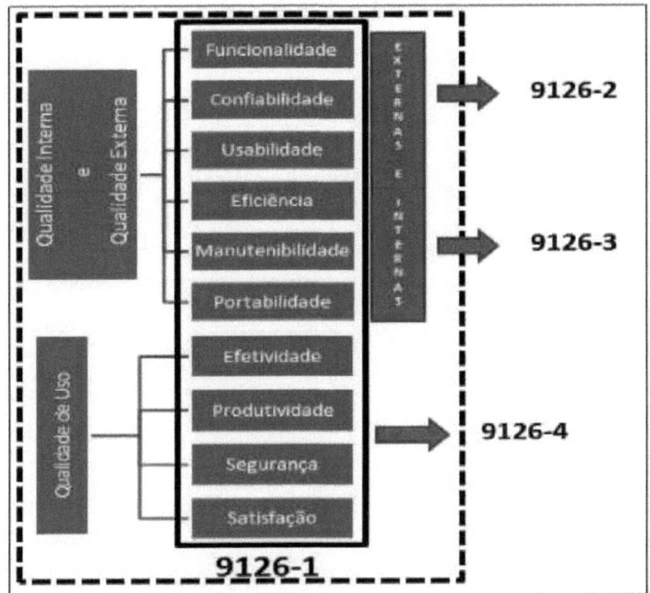

Figura 2.6: Representation of the ISO/IEC 9126 standard. Source: Machado and Souza apud Sodré (2006).

Figura 2.7:

contained in the same set of characteristics, but in an external view. It is this quality that will be assessed while the final *software* product is being tested (Sodré 2006). The Internal and External Quality Model has six basic criteria that define the quality of a *software* product', functionality, reliability, usability, efficiency, maintainability and portability. Figure 2.7 illustrates in detail each sub-criterion to be assessed.

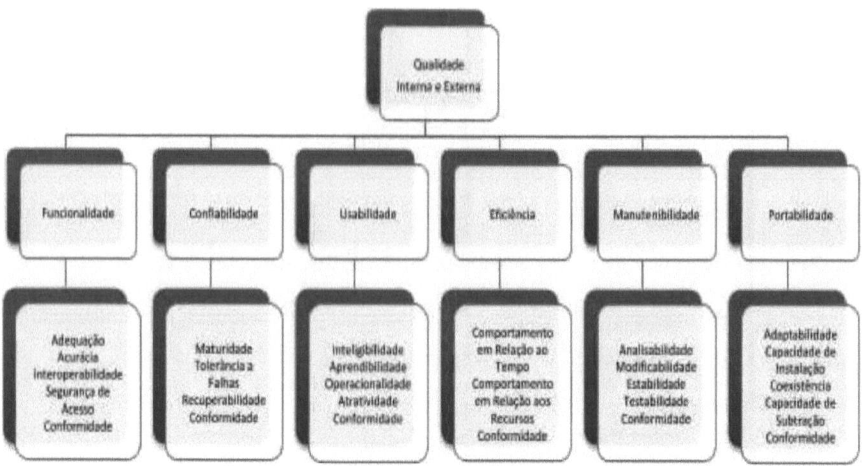

Figura 2.7: External and Internal Quality Characteristics and Sub-Characteristics. Source: Machado and Souza apud Sodré (2006).

The Internal and External Quality Model, shown in Table 2.1, is included in this set of characteristics and will be the basis for the technical assessment of the object of study in question.

The two standards discarded are more focussed on verifying the planning, evaluation and development phases of *software* products, respectively ISO/IEC 14598 and ISO/IEC 9241. The choice of the ISO/IEC 9126 standard was justified by its clear and concise approach to the parameters that meet those desired by the end user of the product.

Therefore, within this context and in accordance with the aforementioned models, the aim of this study is to evaluate the quality of VisuAlg as *software* that supports learning programming. The methodological procedures that subsidised the research are presented below.

Criteria	Description
Functionality	Functionality describes sub-criteria that prove the existence of a set of functions that fulfil explicit or implicit needs and their specific properties.
Reliability	Reliability has a set of attributes that demonstrate the *software*'s ability to maintain its level of performance under established conditions over an established period of time.
Usability	The sub-characteristics of usability or usability show the effort required to be able to use the *software, as well* as the individual judgement of this use, by an implicit or explicit number of users.
Efficiency	The efficiency characteristic is made up of a set of sub-items that verify the relationship between the *software*'s performance level and the amount of resources used, under established conditions.
Maintainability	Maintainability shows the attributes that evaluate the effort required to make specific modifications to the *software*.
Portability	Portability is the ability of *software* to be transferred from one environment to another.

Table 2.1: Technical criteria for assessing *software* quality according to ISO/IEC 9126.

CHAPTER 3

Application of the Case Study

The results of the general objective proposed in this article are presented below. The structure of this section discusses the unfolding of the specific objectives that were delimited earlier and which also addressed the observations that were relevant to achieving the purpose of the research.

3.1 Technical assessment

As mentioned above, this technical evaluation of VisuAlg is based on assigning three levels of acceptance according to the *software's* suitability for the criteria suggested by the ISO/IEC 9126 standard, and showed the following results, as shown in Figure 3.1:

3.1.1 Functionality: HIGH

When we talk about systems development and a functional system, we are defining that *software as having* a behaviour or action that can be visualised with a beginning and an end, something that can be executed.

This execution can be defined as input and output of specific entities or attributes belonging to specific entities (Yamaguti, 2006).

The *software* offers a range of functionalities, including: text editing, pseudocode execution and debugging, step-by-step execution, visualisation of the content of variables, examination of the activation stack in the case of subprogrammes,

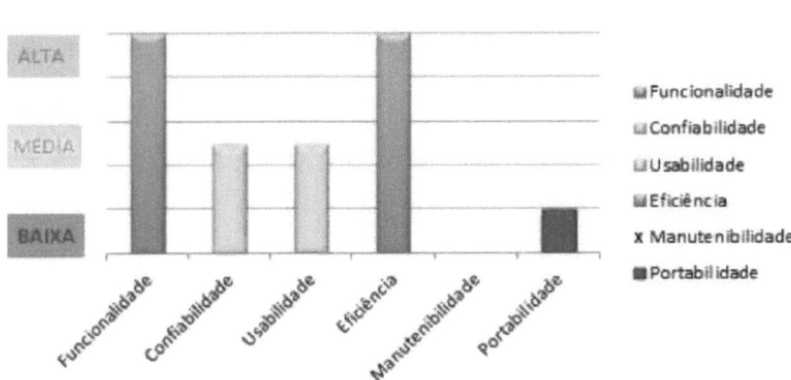

Figure 3.1: Result of the evaluation of the ISO/IEC 9126 technical standard applied to the VisuAlg *software*.

execution counter for each line of the programme, source code generator, among others. These results were extracted after using all the available functions offered by the *software*.

3.1.2 Reliability   : AVERAGE

Reliability is generally defined as the probability that the *software* will operate without faults occurring for a specific period of time in a given environment. It is a multidimensional property that, together with reliability, acts with other factors that determine customer satisfaction, such as functionality, usability, ability to provide service, maintainability and documentation (Silva Filho, 2003). The analysis showed that the *software was* able to maintain a stable level of performance during prolonged use. In addition, there were no serious faults. However, the *software* analysed does not have the capacity to recover data after a system failure, since in the tests the *software* did not save the program after an unexpected system shutdown simulation.

3.1.3   Usability: AVERAGE

Ability to understand, learn, operate and be attractive to the student under specific use.

This concept encompasses four characteristics that are intrinsic to a piece of *software'*, intelligibility, which is the ease with which the student can understand how the *software* works; apprehensibility, which is the ease with which the student can learn to use the product; operability, which is the ease with which the *software can be operated'*, and attractiveness, which is the level of attraction that the *software* causes in the student (Silva Filho, 2003). In the tests there were difficulties in learning some of the *software'*s functionalities at first, such as the correct way to use the execution stack test for the first time. However, with continuous use of the tool, the user gets used to the environment and overcomes the initial difficulties.

3.1.4   Efficiency: HIGH

In the case of *software* products, *this is* when it makes good use of system resources such as memory and processor cycles, including response time, processing time and memory utilisation (Silva Filho, 2003). In analysing this criterion, the *software* has a high efficiency index when subjected to the test that at a given moment, an option in the example code would cause the programme to run in an infinite recursion. The result showed that even in the *loop,* the programme still responded to one of its functionalities. In the execution profile, it was possible to examine the repetitions coming from the *loop,* allowing the user to check the code quickly and objectively.

3.1.5   Maintainability: NOT APPLICABLE

"Ease with which it can be modified to satisfy user requirements or be corrected when deficiencies are found" (Brusamolin, 2004). This criterion is divided into five sub-characteristics: analysability, attributes that diagnose faults or identify parts that can be modified; modifiability, attribute for modifying, removing defects or adapting to changes; stability, attribute that verifies the risks of effects from modifications;

testability, attribute for validating the *software* after modifications; and conformity, attribute for verifying standards and conventions related to portability (Brusamolin, 2004). The *software* is free but not open source, which makes it impossible to analyse its maintainability.

3.1.6 Portability: LOW

Ability to compile and run on different *hardware* and *software* architectures. It has sub-characteristics such as: adaptability, the ability to adapt to different environments without the need to apply other actions; the ability to be installed in a specific environment; coexistence, sharing common resources with other *software* products', *the* ability to replace, which can be used to replace other specific *software* with the same purpose and in the same environment; and compliance related to portability, acting in accordance with standards and conventions related to portability (Gomes Filho, 2005). In this evaluation, the tests showed that the *software* is only available for the Microsoft® Windows operating system in its 98, Millennium, 2000 and XP versions, restricting the use of the *software* to more up-to-date systems.

3.2 Pedagogical evaluation

The pedagogical evaluation of VisuAlg consists of subjectively analysing the criteria based on the Reeves model (1994). The observation resulted in the following model shown in Figure 3.2.

3.2.1 Instructional sequencing: Reductionist/Constructivist

The model proposed by Reeves points to a balance between reductionism, which favours learning based on prior knowledge of the system's components, and constructionism, indicating that knowledge should be explored according to the student's needs within the usability of the tool, placing them within a realistic context in which they will require solutions to the problems suggested. In fact, it is not possible to fully utilise the system without first getting to know some basic functionalities that will help with future inferences about learning development.

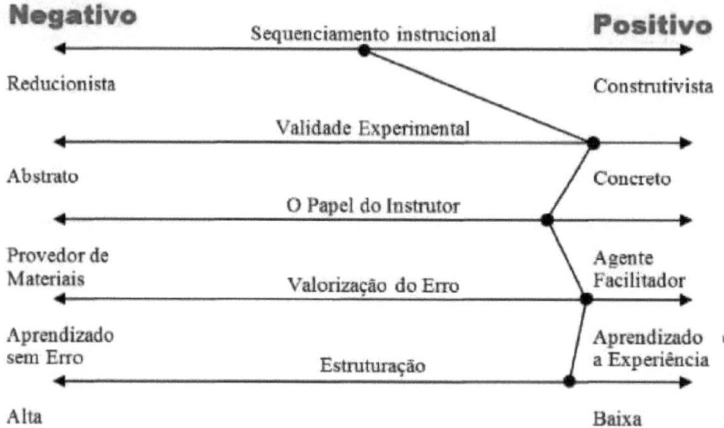

Figure 3.2: Model resulting from Reeves' pedagogical evaluation applied to the Vi-suAlg *software*.

3.2.2 **Experimental validity: Concrete**

It makes it possible to contextualise the content presented to the student with the intention of offering real situations that are the "minimum necessary in terms of control, measurement, analysis and procedures that make it possible to interpret the results of the experiment" (Santo, 1992). With this in mind, the test consisted of observing whether the execution profile and activation stack functionalities provided a more concrete examination of the execution of the code and the exchange of variable content, respectively.

3.2.3 **Role of the Instructor: Facilitator**

In this way, cognitive responsibility is transferred to the students, as they become responsible for judging patterns of information, organising data, constructing new alternatives and presenting new knowledge (Reeves, 1994). The teacher then takes on the role of a source of guidance, consultation and generator of coordinated problem situations with the aim of favouring and facilitating student learning. Tests indicate that the teacher is interfering less and less in the student's decisions, given the autonomy that the student acquires as learning progresses.

3.2.4 Valuing Error: Learning from Experience

With the forms of debugging available in the programme, such as the activation stack, the execution profile and the three execution modes available, the student can choose the best way to understand their errors, which may be created intentionally, as was possible to simulate in the tests, helping them to understand some detail intrinsic to the code, thus providing experiences that will make learning more dynamic.

3.2.5 Structuring: Low

The *software is* not very structured, as students don't need to follow sequential steps to build their knowledge of how to use it. They can choose, for example, to learn the commands available in the menus in order to use the *software* more accurately, or they can skip this step and their use and understanding won't be compromised, i.e. they can choose the order they want to follow in the *software.*

CHAPTER 4

Results and Discussion

In the technical evaluation, the *software* showed a high performance in the functionality criterion, as it offers an easy language with basic and clear functions that don't require adi citional definitions, and efficiency precisely because of the ease of the language, which provides the user with faster responses. In terms of reliability, the *software* performed satisfactorily because it didn't have any serious faults during prolonged use, even though it couldn't recover data in the event of a system failure. As for usability, the user may initially encounter some difficulties, which can be overcome by continuous use of the tool.

In the pedagogical assessment, in the two criteria analysed, the model points to a balance that can be considered necessary within the educational context. Analysing the *software* in instructional sequencing suggests both a reductionist factor, as it requires a prior understanding of the content in order to advance in learning, and a cons- trutivist factor, as it places the student in a realistic context, which requires solving problems according to their subjective needs.

With regard to the other aspects, the *software* also achieved satisfactory results, working as a facilitator and not merely as a support for "content transfer". We can say that VisuAlg thus favours efficient learning by prioritising the acquisition of experience through the study and visualisation of errors.

CHAPTER 5

Conclusions

In view of the difficulties encountered at the start of learning programming, it is recommended that the usual teaching be reviewed and that the use of pedagogical tools be analysed and expanded, with the aim of gradually improving student performance and, consequently, effectively reducing the dropout rate caused by this factor. In these circumstances, VisuAlg achieves the goals it sets out to achieve, bringing it closer to the day-to-day reality of a programmer's work and enabling learning through knowledge and understanding of the mistakes made throughout the process of building algorithms.

Based on the analysis of the VisuAlg *software* carried out in item 4, it can be concluded that this tool allows students who are new to programming courses to exercise their knowledge in an environment that is close to reality, satisfying the motivational aspects that make learning more productive, without the formality of a programming language that requires greater dedication on the part of the students. Something that, for them, is a reason for giving up and/or difficulty in progressing with their learning.

Thus, contextualising the results obtained after applying the pedagogical methods of Reeves (1994) and the technical methods of the Internal and External Quality model of the ISO/IEC 9126 standard, a satisfactory result was obtained from the pedagogical point of view, although the *software did* not meet all the technical criteria assessed. It needs to be improved in terms of portability, as it only offers compatibility with one operating system and is only available for four versions considered to be old.

The evaluations showed that the *software* can be classified as educational, as it obtained positive scores on the pedagogical model evaluation scale, and that even though it has shortcomings in terms of portability, its technical evaluation is also favourable, as its usability, reliability and efficiency are not compromised. It is therefore hoped that more extensive studies will be proposed and carried out so that the effectiveness of educational *software* such as VisuAlg in the teaching-learning process can be proven, helping teachers in their teaching role, thus providing a clearer and more concise education in the objects studied.

Bibliography

AGUIAR, E. V. (2008). **New Technologies and Teaching and Learning.** Vértices, V. 10, n. 1/3.

ALVES, J. C., SAMPAIO, L. C., CARVALHO, M. C., ALDEIA, S. F., GUELPELI, A. C., & GUELPELI, M. V. (2004). **Methodology for Evaluating Authoring** *Software* **as a Computational Tool to Assist in the Development of Didactic-Pedagogical Content.** Volta Redonda - RJ: Fluminense Federal University.

BERTOLDI, S. **Evaluation of Educational** *Software*: **Impressions and Reflections.** Federal University of Santa Catarina. Florianópolis, 1999.

BRANDÃO, E. J. (1998). **Rethinking Educational** *Software* **Evaluation Models.** Passo Fundo - RS: University of Passo Fundo.

BRUSAMOLIN, V. *Software* **Maintainability.** Scientific Institute of Higher Education and Research - ICESP. Online Digital Magazine Vol 2 - January 2004.

FERREIRA, T. A., MOREIRA, R. C., & MOZZAQUATRO, P. M. (2011). **Quality Assessment of Educational** *Software.* XVI Interinstitutional Seminar on Teaching, Research and Extension.

FRESCKI, F. B; **Evaluation of the Quality of Educational** *Software* **for Teaching Algebra.** Monograph, Cascavel-PR. UEOP, 2008.

GAMA, C. L. G; **Method for the Construction of Learning Objects with Application to Numerical Methods.** PhD Thesis, Curitiba-PR. UFPR, 2007.

GIL, A. **C. Como elaborar projetos de pesquisa.** São Paulo: Atlas, 2006. Available at <http://www.proppi.uff.br/turismo/sites/default/files/como_elaborar_projeto_de_pesq uisa_oc o_antnio_carlos_gil.pdf >. Accessed on 17 November 2012.

GLADCHEFF, A. P; DA SILVA, D.M; MALDONADO, J. C. **Diretrizes para um Instrumento de Avaliação de Qualidade para** *Software de* **Ensino.** Workshop of theses in *software* engineering, Florianópolis, SC, Brazil. Proceedings, pages 18-22,1999.

GOMES FILHO, M. J. A. **A Process for Evaluating the Portability of** *Software* **Units.** Federal University of Pernambuco. Computer Centre, Recife - PE. 2004.

INTERNATIONAL ORGANISATION FOR STANDARDIZATION. **ISO 9241:** Available at: <http://www.iso.org/iso/home/store/catalogue_tc/catalogue_detail.htm?csnumber=53 59 0> Accessed on: 14 Nov. 2012.

INTERNATIONAL ORGANISATION FOR STANDARDIZATION. **ISO 9126:** Available at: <http://www.iso.org/iso/home/store/catalogue_tc/catalogue_detail.htm7csnumberf97 5 2>. Accessed on: 14 November 2012.

INTERNATIONAL ORGANISATION FOR STANDARDIZATION. **ISO 14598:** Available at: <http://www.iso.org/iso/home/store/catalogue_tc/catalogue_detail.h tm7cs number=24907>. Accessed on: 14 November 2012.

LUCENA, M. (1998). **Guidelines for Training Teachers in Educational Technology:** Criteria for Evaluating Educational *Software.* Virtual Journal of Educational Informatics and Distance Education - Educadi - CE.

MACHADO, M. P.; SOUZA, S. F. **Metrics and** *Software* **Quality.** Available at: <http://www.fattocs.com.br/download/qualidade-sw.pdf>. Accessed on: 14 Nov. 2012.

MARCONI, M. A; LAKATOS, E. M. **Técnicas de pesquisa.** Atlas, 6th Edition, 2007.

NESBIT, J.; BELFER, K.; VARGO, J. **A Convergent Participation Model for Evaluation of Learning Objects.** Canadian Journal of Leaming and Technology, v.28(3), 2002. Available at: <http://www.cjlt.ca/content/vol28.3/nesbit_etal.htm>. Accessed on: 13 Nov. 2012.

NIELSEN, J. **Ten Usability heuristics.** Available at: <http://www.useit.com/papers/ heuristic/heuristic_list.html>. Accessed on: 13 Nov. 2012.

NOBRE, I. A. M; MENEZES, C. S. **Support for Co-operation in a Learning Environment for Programming (SAmbA).** XIII Brazilian Symposium on Informatics in Education - SBIE - UNISINOS, 2002.

PÍCCOLO, H. L. et al. **Interactive and Adaptable Environment for Teaching Programming.** XXI Brazilian Symposium on Informatics in Education. 4, 28,2010.

PMBOK Guide. **A Guide to the Project Management Body of Knowledge.** Project Management Institute. 4 ed. Pennsylvania-USA, 2008.

PRESSMAN, R. S. *Software* **Engineering.** Translated by Rosângela Delloso Penteado. São Paulo: McGraw-Hill, 2006.

RAMOS, E. **O Fundamental na Avaliação da Qualidade do *Software* Educacional. Educational** *Software* Laboratory - EDUGRAF. Department of Computer Science and Statistics. Federal University of Santa Catarina, 2003.

REEVES, T. **Systematic Evaluation Procedures for Interactive Multimedia for Education and Training.** Multimedia computing: preparing for the 21st century. Harrisburg, PA. Idea Group, 1994.

ROCHA, A. R; CAMPOS, G. H, B. **Quality Evaluation of Educational *Software*.** Em Aberto. Brasília, v. 12, n. 57, p. 32-44,1993.

SANTO, A. E. **Delineamentos de Metodologia Científica.** Loyola Editions. São Paulo. P. 169,1992.

SILVA FILHO, A. M. *Software* **Reliability Engineering.** Department of Computer Science. State University of Maringá - PR. 2003. Available at: <http://www.espacoacademico.com.br/027/27amsf.htm> Accessed on: 21 Jan. 2013.

SILVA, C. R., & VARGAS, C. L. **Avaliação da Qualidade de *Software* Educacional.**

Rio de Janeiro: XIX Encontro Nacional de Engenharia de Produção and V International Congress of Industrial Engineering, 1999.

SODRÉ, C. C. P. **Norma ISO/IEC 9126: Avaliação de Qualidade de Produtos de** *Software.*
State University of Londrina. Londrina, 2006.

SOMMERVILLE, I. F. *Software* **Engineering.** Translated by Selma Shin Shimiza Melnikoff, Reginaldo Arakaki and Edilson de Andrade Barbosa. São Paulo: Addison-Wesley, 2007.

SOUZA, C. M. **VisuAlg - Tool to Support Programming Teaching.** Severino Sombra University, CECETEN. TECCEN Magazine, vol. 2 n. 2 September 2009 [S.l], 2009.

TAKAHASHI, T. **Information Society in Brazil:** Green Book. Brasília: Ministry of Science and Technology, 2000.

TOMAZ, M. F. *Softwares* **Educacionais e o Ensino de História: Elementos para uma análise didática.** Master's dissertation in Education. Federal University of Paraná. Curitiba, 2005.

FEDERAL UNIVERSITY OF PARANÁ. **Pedagogical Evaluator.** EEHouse - The House of Energy Efficiency. UFPR, 2009. Available at :< http://www.design.ufpr.br/lai/arquivos/EEHouse_1_AvalPedagogico.pdf >. Accessed on 15 Nov. 2012.

VALENTE, J. A. **The Computer in the Knowledge Society.** Campinas: UNICAMP/NIED, 1999.

YAMAGUTI, S. Y. **Object Orientation in Systems Development: Concepts and Characteristics.** Open School of Brazil. Brasília-DF. 2006.

Printed by Books on Demand GmbH, Norderstedt / Germany